Poems of Lament & Grace

Dorothy Lee's *Poems of Lament and Grace* is a book rich in times and seasons, reaching back to classical Greece and reaching out to embrace 'all the vastness' found between ordinary letters and 'the depths / of love and plenitude and silence'. These are poems that probe the struggles that fill our lives of faith and questioning, of hope and weariness. To read a lyric such as 'Sea Monster' is to be changed forever.

Kevin Hart
The University of Virginia

These poems are vivid with feeling and intellect. They pattern a call and response between the poet and her world, both inner and outer, with rhythms that fall into the natural pattern of speech even as the ideas take us to the infinitely great and the infinitely small. A book of poems to read aloud, to see the world anew, to question the heart of language, and to savour again.

Katherine Firth
The University of Melbourne

Poems of Lament & Grace

Dorothy Lee

Published in Australia by
Coventry Press
33 Scoresby Road
Bayswater VIC 3153

ISBN 9781922589446

Catalogue-in-Publication entry is available from the National Library of Australia
http://catalogue.nla.gov.au

Cover design by Ian James – www.jgd.com.au
Cover photograph by Bradley Cummings
www.bradleycummingsphotography.com.au
Text design by Coventry Press
Set in Tex Gyre Pagella

Printed in Australia

for
Miriam Edith and Irene Mary

Contents

Foreword

On the very first page of this collection, we read about 'the vastness in between/ the lettering'. One way or another, this is a recurrent motif: the vastness of a promise in and behind words, to which the words can only gesture; and the vastness of an inner landscape where it's hard not to feel utterly abandoned, waiting (as one of these poems puts it) for the farmer/shepherd to remember that somewhere out there is a voice enquiring with desperation, a desperation born from the sense of sheer disconnectedness from everything that might make human sense.

The poem entitled 'Lament' opens out from this, moving subtly from the opening 'He never was incarnate in your flesh', the flat denial that God can be believed to have shared the flesh of the really and unmendably broken (the imagery has fresh and shocking resonance as we look at pictures of what is happening in Ukraine) to the enigmatic conclusion, 'he never *seemed* incarnate in your flesh'.

As we are reminded, the one who inhabits that 'vastness' along with you is playing a long game (the title of another poem). The surface of desolation is being slowly unsettled by a steady shift in the depths. As we hear in 'Sea Monster', something shares our inner ocean, and pushes through in ways and places we could not predict. Navigating or negotiating with this unfathomable sea (and its divine wildlife) is another regular motif in the world of these poems.

Any poetry that tries to speak honestly and freshly out of the journey of faith will be a poetry of loss, not only of celebration, and these poems do full justice to that, never shirking the tracklessness of the land or the sea where the journey is taking us. The late mediaeval German contemplative writers like Tauler and Suso relished the language of a journey without landmarks and a language 'without why' (*ohne warum*), unmoored from explanation and organization. But the celebration arises out of just this tracklessness, and there are some beautiful affirmations here of environment and family, sacramental vision and re-founded hope.

A poetry of faith in this sense is persuasive and credible to the extent that it doesn't let you forget where it came from in human terms, the anger and chaos and lostness, and yet doesn't seek to make an edifying pattern out of this ('You're having a dreadful time but it will get better'). It never strays too far from the vastness, in which is both unmitigated danger and unexplainable transfiguration. These poems beautifully and honestly inhabit that territory, swim in those waters. And again, like any good poetry of faith, they tell us not to be afraid if this is the territory where we find ourselves.

Bishop Rowan Williams

Preface

These poems span two decades of my life, during which I have taught, researched and studied, preached and celebrated the sacraments. They have been times where my life has been surrounded by the towering (and sometimes ambiguous) structures of church and university. Within them. my own journey has played out its own narrative: sometimes drawing comfort, sometimes in rebellion, and sometimes faltering and uncertain. These poems — as the title suggests — represent moments of both divine absence and presence. Yet doubt and lament belong within the wider context of faith: the awareness of that grace which sees and welcomes our responses, good or bad, strong or weak, confident or vulnerable.

I owe a number of thanks: to Bradley Cummings whose photo of the steps on Mt Catherine partly inspired the poem 'Transfiguration'; to my sister, Ruth Lee Martin, who encouraged me and set to music the poem 'Annunciation' and who, as a composer, is the inspiration for 'This Place of Sound'; to Peter Campbell, for setting to music 'Christmas Afternoon'; to my friends and colleagues, Muriel Porter and Christiaan Mostert, for their kindly responsiveness to my writing over many years; to my grandchildren (Jemina, Theodore, Harriet, Wilfred) who may one day read this book; and lastly to my daughters, Miriam and Irene, to whom this book is dedicated, for their capacity to interpret poetry and make it come alive.

December 2023

1

Newer Poems

Alchemy

Even a shopping list
seems near enough some days:

the need to clutch a pen
or splay your fingers on an alphabet,
the pages flickering on an ashen screen —

anything to conjure mortal words
that start and end,
and maybe swell to something in the middle;
unfinal though you know each one,
hardly the form you dreamed,

  but good enough to make you muse
  on all the vastness in between
  the lettering,

and God, who always scribes in perfect uncials
in discourse far and near,
each utterance an unimagined deed —

turning your ill-formed copy
into liquid prose
your base-born metals
into gold.

Birthday

Today they seem so numerous,
the years,
tumbling over in my head,
spinning out heat and wet and winter
in season after season,

expanding nights and days
in blurred receding
loops that swirl
to the horizon's rim.

Uncountable, unaccountable,
surprising me at every turn
(where they came from, when they left),
that I should reach this
place of rounding,
this arithmetic sum
that marks impeccably the years?

And yet from still another view
so few, so thinly spread.
As if their history could be written
on a page without a word,
a line, a syllable left out.

On other days without the sums,
without the calculations
it seems the waters that I tread defy
the years -
as if I float, an infant, in a warm,
ecstatic pool that has no ocean floor:

only the depths
of love and plenitude and silence.

Christmas Afternoon

Tired by the journey and mortal toil,
the whisper of outraged clan,
you sit on a corner of dusty hay,
dazed by the warmth of the barn.

The sun streams in through the fissured door
the drowsy silence waits.
Bush-fire and drought, you've seen them all come
in by the open gate.

No-one sees you and nobody heeds,
they're all in census rows.
Shepherds now gone and star-men late,
    your body too slight to hold this grant of gold.

Just for a moment you sense a stir
out of the side of an eye:
a fluttering wind, a distant whirr,
    a silver feather dances at your side.

Labour

It was toil for me.

Not just the usual parts —
pain beyond pain,
loveliness thrust in brittle arms —

but much of the journey afterwards:
    the unaccountable days,
    the waking nights,
    the chafing limitations.

But different now for you.

You sit in the armchair with your son,
your long hair falling over
the breast on which
the small dark head is laid;
    eyes appraising what you do:
    as if it were an arduous yet pleasing
    reverie.

I can't aspire to labour such as yours,
but in my heart today
there isn't room for envy or regret —
    only the knowledge of you
    in this beguiling guise.

Dust / Easter

Everything at last to dust:
these quilted veins,
ribbons grained in sturdy flesh,
the budded leaf,
the curve of summer wing and feather;
the breath of morning
or grasses' sway in evening air;

all flakes of dust
in wind-born haze,
fragments of fading memory.

Meaning is such a tiring business,
a struggle you know you're bound to lose.
Not at first, not in the day-to-day;

but in the place where all roads end,
and crowds recede,
where foliage begins to droop:
flecks of grim caught on the last horizon.

Yet when the dust has settled,
there's always Easter
year after spinning year,
a shimmer on the edge of nothingness.

When the blackened limbs have gone,
after the second burial,
then there's a new remembering:
ossuaries cracked like broken shells,
bone transmuted into new-born flesh.

Latest of all, the voice of an only Child
utters a final yes
above the desert's deafening roar.

Question-mark

A little here, a little there,
not really here, not truly there:
Where do I belong?

Most days the question hangs in the air:
sometimes in bright sunlight fading
like hazy smoke or skywriting;

other times circled in black lines
across a winter sky
mirrored on soft interior walls
and cosy furnishings,

echoing doubts
that seem to speak an undying word of
disconnect.

Yet not a quest
for me to answer or resolve:

this one is yours.
Your shadow lurking
within the punctuation
even as it slowly curls in upon itself:

Your circle to sustain the failing lines,
to make the crooked straight,

and forge a path
across a semantic wilderness.

Lament

He never was incarnate in your flesh.

You crept around the outskirts of his realm.
invisible against the glistening sand:
    as if the sun were burning in his eyes
    each time he looked your way.

The men around him, shrouded in heavy clothes,
obeyed his outstretched hand
    the focused gaze,
    the strong imperious finger.
They heard the whisper of his voice,
the dazzling god he placed within the cradle of their hands.

He understood their life:
    the mortal clay, the lilies of the field.

You could not claim his likeness as your own;
    you never heard him knocking at your door;
    you never saw the glitter of his lamp.

You did not greet him in your home:
    the broken glass,
    the gaping walls,
    the traces of lost paradise.

He never seemed incarnate in your flesh.

(for Luce Irigaray)

Bedside

I sit beside your bed
gazing down upon you:
	mouth half-open,
	eyelids closed,
	the laboured in-and-out of breath,
	the tightening of your chest.

Whether you are ready to depart
I hardly know,
suspecting that whatever it is
you are at peace,
though I think you'd rather stay

not just for those of us
you love
across three generations

but most of all for her,
whose voice you've heard each day
from a distant isle:
	the lonely Hebridean moors,
	the standing stones,
	a mystic tongue
	pushed to the edge of land and sea.

Beside your bed
these thoughts and memories arise.
I can't reach out to you to name them:
your spirit is already almost gone
winging its way to yet another island,
	a distant country
	far beyond our ken.

Restraint and Grace

Restraint and grace:
how cordially they stand together:
        as if you too could walk
        into the sunlit clearing,
        into the circle of their amity.

Knowing instead your incapacity
to be so godlike,

nor give the benefit
to that narrow-minded other
who settles down complacently
beside the water's edge,
        rippling through the stillness
        in words of jagged stone.

In place of mild sagacity
you fire fierce sparks of ire,

kindling an inadvertent flame
in the encircling grasses.

Long Game

I'm not sure I like
this tendency of yours
to play a waiting game —

    the years of silence, absence, dearth
    (whatever you want to call it)
    when you weren't there;

and I assumed indifference,
or sometimes non-existence.

But now I begin to wonder,
remembering those harder times,
if there was nothing
even you could do:

    nothing to stem the fears
    that tumbled over each another
    in rising waves;

and I was adrift on unfamiliar seas —
community, love, vocation —
without the sight of homecoming.

Nothing to do but await
the measured passing of the years:
to reach this welcome place

and find you after all
its architect.

Parakeets

We were talking in the kitchen
yesterday,

or rather you were musing
in one of your rare monologues,
didactic in its scope,

when a harsh note intruded
from the garden.

A frown swept over your face;
you raised your intonation as if to quell it —
a clamorous schoolroom.

After you'd gone
(fading to your usual inwardness),
the same discordant sound recurred,
in echoing squawks.
I walked outside in early evening,
the sun still tingling in the fading heat,

    to see a flock of parakeets
    swooping from tree to tree,
    plumped out feathers and yellow plumes,
    insensible to neighbours and to noise.

The larrikins of the aviatic world, I thought,
revving their battered sportscars up and down the street,
    music blaring from their open panes.

Later that night I thought of you again, considering
the girl I knew through younger years
in adolescent walks:
then, careful and regarding,
assessing the world with opaque stare;
now, knowing and more decorous
in very different, graceful flight across
the glittering skies.

Good Friday

Heaven muddles good and bad,
hardly knowing fine distinctions.
A day of death is held as glad,
        with woeful rites and chanted jeremiad.

True that faithful women reach the tomb,
gazing on life and death transformed:
        the third for them, a wondrous celebration.

But bad for me and mine, oh yes,
for this day wills to mirror me,
        turns me to look at what I like the least.

Some are above who disagree,
holding celestial time and place,
        a higher, topsy-turvy world than I can see:

'Death be not proud', they laughing say:
'the bad is good, the good is bad'.
        And flutter through another looking-glass.

Critic

I remember the day
the tiger was unleashed.

Displeasure crouching
behind his wooden desk,
syllables outlining
        your ignorance
        and failure.

Too late to change the tune,
bartering contrite words.
The wildcat had escaped its bars,
the haunches hurtling through
the door;

the pointed claws affording little
mercy.

Since then you manage in a sullen kind of way:
        some days by camouflage,
        others forgetting that it lurks in coverts,
        in patches of orange hue,

but sooner or later
stalking your paths, prepared once more to pounce:
        the canines bared,
        a lashing tail.

Can anyone constrain this predatory hunt —
or stem the anger rising up against
        your own collusion?

Even the memory elongates
its presence,
pacing the floor with fretful recollections.

Winter Vigil

A stubborn winter swirls about the place,
mirroring the turmoil of our feelings
as we stand beside this peaceful, unmoved man,
    the flesh receding day by day,
    the face more gaunt,
    the sunken eyes,
    the thinness of his frame.

How hard for us to wait and watch,
to hold the reins on grief and keep
the vigil of this parting.

He shaped the contours of our lives:
the faith, the certainty, the depth;
sometimes a little too hard to bear.

In later years
we skirted round division
and held to common ground,
discovering breaches in his certainties.

We liked the kindness
and the humour,
the warmth and thoughtful spirit —
forged in the suffering
of the early years.

We liked the passion of his principles,
the sense of gazing into depths
that others failed to see,
the love of words
both human and divine.

How difficult now to wait upon his timing,
and face this wintry loss —
to offer up his spirit (with our own)
to what the future may or may not hold.

Circles

I never divined the presence of a third
until you mentioned it this morning,
as if you thought it obvious.

I knew quite well the other circles:
the years inhabiting their enclosures:
        the one with wavering lines,
        uncertain of its shape and hue;
        the other firm and knowing,
        a narrow, gilded sphere.

And now you claim to see a third
weaving mysterious paths between the two,

striving to make a mark
on territory unflagged:
        a rounded lake,
        a curve of water,
        a tangled crown of foliage,

Within the dimming earth
this is an ocean I might learn to navigate —

thanks to your faith that I could love the spin
of crescent moons,
glinting like silver on the fluted waves.

Seamstress

In dreams you conceive things otherwise:

imagine yourself in coloured garb
made up of woven strands
whose cloth you've cut out and stitched:
taking your place by right of craft
at this hard-working table.

But in ordinary life,
you never can be sure
of something that might follow you:
unpicking stitches,
snipping rents,
fading the pigment.

Perhaps one day
some nimble-fingered seamstress
will gather all the fragments:
shaping and sewing to make a robe
more radiant
than anything you could dream.

Transfiguration

Beyond seeing
the peak recedes above you in the dusky lights,
the incline sharpening to a cross of ragged bone,
hostile to each intrepid hold
of pick or rope:
arduous to scale the glittering heights.

Nearer to hand and eye
the foothills dance like commoners
beneath imperial slopes
that clutch perhaps reluctantly their dignity.

On one side you note the ruins of a stair,
half-hidden by a round of scrub,
ascending upwards to a broken arch,
ensnaring twilight in the darkening air.

while deep on the southern side,
you shy from a chasm hacked from a hidden lair,
plunging its gradients to the Underworld
from where the river Jordan springs
forlornly in the chilly air.

Secret and safe upon the lower zones,
a cavern facing inwards gives you shelter,
an opening hard to find on dismal days:
    the merest blot,
    a blemish in the soil,
    the grasses striving with the pitted stones;

from where you notice daily an occurrence
the ascent of travellers on this far-flung tower
        whose feet,
        whose panting breath,
        whose dampened forehead
        surge expectantly past your hidden bower.

And some time later in the eventide,
you find yourself awake and standing in the opening,
peering half-sleepy into a mandorla
where cold stars glint above the mountainside:

wondering whether you dreamed the burst of flame
or felt the ages in your breast uncoil
or heard for a flickering moment far away
the sound of distant thunder calling out your name.

2

Older Poems

Annunciation

Yours was the first:
the home, the cradle,
adolescent nest of flesh and bone,
lined all around with down and feathers
or mulch of leaves mellowed in autumn airs,
ready to hail the quickening buried seed.

Yours was the sited sanctuary,
incense and fire burned on parchment plans,
cloud and thurible, altar and hearth,
a bird of paradise free to roam
unheeding through your oaken beams.

Yours was the layering of sunlit stone,
built on foundations forged in rocky soil
while, far within, an architect
measures the contours of both guest and host
pacing with untried feet the flag-stone paths;

till fed from a common bowl
you reach across the wooden board,
clasping divisions first and last—
the faltering steps and banished pangs of Eve.

And then the hour of dawn.
A perfect form through window-pane and keyhole,
gathering speed on aisles of singing angels,
squeezing his thin, apologetic limbs
between the cleft of rock
as daytime darkens into evening
and lights of myriad stars begin to wink.

The watchman waiting
stammers out the hours,
hearkens the muted cry in three-fold darkness,
beholds the bloody cloths and streaming breast,
the dark hair damp against your forehead,

knowing you hold in wearied hands
the world.

Threshold

I. In the end it was harder than I thought:
seated on plastic chairs in the waiting room
shackled together in coloured rows,
        the lino grey and polished,
        the bench-tops of stainless steel,
        and a scaling for weights like a door-mat;
        the glass doors sliding in opposite directions
on flushed and open faces.

Then after the choice is made,
to fall asleep securely on my lap
as if there isn't a care in the world,
only the binding of touch and skin and fur —
just as it always used to be;

gainsaying for a moment the reason we're here:
        the dead, unwinking eyes,
        staring for hours at faceless walls,
        or knocking against bewildered doors,
        his rough voice lifting in lamentation.

II. The fluid in the blood is burnished green,
like medicine for a child or venom of snakes
tipped on a fiery dart:
subduing his heart with too disarming an ease;
sending him off to an ill-defined location
without the pious comforts we're allowed.
        My hands rest briefly on his face
        tracing a sign across his forehead.

And now like a stone
he stretches across the table in an empty room,
the eyes half open declining to be closed
as if in protest at the day he left us,
dwelling in darkness of his own domain.

When at last he's gathered up in other arms,
after the final parting,
    his head droops over like a newborn child,
    and I imagine for a moment he's neatly folded
    his life away like a blanket.

Tsunami

It's harder than ever
to believe in you:

fountain of living water,
drink for the thirsty,
morning dew
on leaves and flowers,
rainfall in the desert,
tinkling streams across the valleys:
source of all bliss and spring-time.

Yet now it seems
also the source
of a single crack in the carcass of the world,
lifting the billowing seas,
and a wave more dreadful
than Noah's —

but no ark to lift them
singly or in pairs to safety;
no rescue for the mother
torn from her children,
no river riven for the dead to cross,
nothing for the infant
but a floating tomb on an angry surge.

From your high window
far above the vehement waters,
did you ever once look out

to behold the insolent breach
of your boundaries?

Wilderness

I inhabit these days a landscape
where nothing seems to protect:
    no cave or den,
    no glimpse of an oasis,
    only a sea of sand on every side, shifting from heat to cold
    a cycle of endless incompletion.

Out in this known yet unknown place,
it's not the solitude I fear,
but something worse:
a kind of disconnected darkness,
    no thread that binds,
    no covering or lover's arms,
    all knowledge of a dreaming centre lost.

Night after night I await the farmer,
hoping that just once more
    he might abandon the ninety-nine
    and set off in the darkness for the wilderness.

Narration

I awake this morning
to a sick, solitary bounding of the heart,
as if the hearing of my case were already lost.

Why is it that, no matter how I try,
I can never be the centre
of a narrative:
not mine or anybody else's?

I live my life on the borders of your garden,
never substantial enough to see you
on your evening ramble,
never holding your godly gaze,
never sure the leafy cloth
will not blow aside or tear,
        exposing nakedness and shame,
        unwitting stolen fruit:
        an allegory undeciphered.

I'm not confident in knowing, as others do,
that a story unfolds
within and around them.
Yet what I desire in all the world
is such a paradisal anecdote —
with you, of course, the storyteller —
enfolding all the fragments of my being,
        flesh turned backwards into word,
        body enraptured into spirit:
        bestowing a pre-existent narrative upon me,
        a leaping heart

to recount the tale
of my vindication
in your skilful narrator's hands.

Railroad

Then there were the frozen years:
the in-between times
that lasted almost a third

of my life's labour;
        and a row of cottages
        on a dead-end street without faces,
        and the children, living and dead,
        and the smell of fear
        almost every night before I slept,
        and a liquid amber
        stretching bare arms across a winter sky.

Only I knew
how cracked the cisterns were,
how dried up the waters at their source.
For everyone else, including the very nearest
(as I discovered, if you remember,
when it fell apart) —
it seemed a fecund valley,
a narrative of aptitude and inclination.

I lived apart in a far-off land,
haemorrhaging selfhood like an open purse,
        sitting by the railroad eating husks,
        and watching the years the locusts ate
        slowly, inexorably rolling by.

Painted Dolls

Six of them hang
from various points about the room,
poised at peculiar angles
over window-sill and railing.

Painted in childish or angelic shades:
    the faceless orb,
    the body bound in straw,
    the wing-span frayed,
    the belly tapering
    to a sudden point.

They're her idea
though she professes no belief —
brought from the market
with pots of primary paint
and gold and silver grey.

We concentrate around the table,
mostly in silence,
sometimes a breath of laughter at our mother's hands,
    a little gnarled, with careless smudges
    clenching the long thin brush;
    her work a memory of returning tides
    tossing us back to infancy.

I paint in gold and green,
daubing along frail lines of wing and feather,
while creatures far beyond my ken
for all I know
dance on a thousand pins of summer light:

hailing the meeting long ago
    a wing-tip in the flare of day,
    a garden bower torn,
    the petals bruised on footless paths.

Now Advent's closer than it's gone,
and still the stilted figures dangle —
swinging forlorn in early spring,
their gaze transfixed upon the glass

awaiting a word, a look, an expiration,
anything at all to indicate
the chance
of correlation.

This Place of Sound

The woman sits before the open keys.
The light streams in through linear blinds,
slanting on black or white
and on the patchwork colours of her hair.
        Outside the summer croons,
        now hot, now fresh and cool.
She likes it better in the heat,
her oval face dissecting warmth,
spectacles perched on the edge of a stubborn nose.

The branches sway in temperate breezes,
magpies call across the emerald lawn,
the traffic hums beyond the walls.

She needs it peaceful, in and out:
        no sudden move,
        no noise beyond the everyday,
        no tactless interloper;
even the dogs have found by intuition
that this is no time for play,
and loll serene and placid round her feet.

Her brow is furrowed,
green eyes stare into a distant land
inhabited not by populace and vegetation
but soft interior sound,
from time to time reflected
on the naked score beneath her gaze.

Her problem is too many not too few,
and how to keep them near and yet at bay,
and how each moves according to some other:
        a blur of triplets, steady march of minims,
        clusters of quavers,
        rests and rallentandos;
each floating in the air above her head,
while jewelled fingers wander to and fro
seeking to find them bed and board:
a dwelling fit to compass them.

Yet deep within each possibility,
though miles from any shore,
she strains to catch the echo of the ocean,
        the pounding of the waves upon the rocks
        swirling past islands veiled in mist
        and mountains cleaving rain-filled clouds —
a melody
beyond the reach of ear or eye,
but hidden in the truest composition.

Sea Monster

I think a monster's swimming in my sea.

Admittedly, I'm never sure of it:
        sometimes a swirling of the waves,
        sometimes an arrow cleaving paths
        across the swell;
        sometimes a glimpse of blue-grey hump,
while schools of lesser fish
dive with abandon to the ocean floor.

It brings to mind no dance
        of silver-bellied whale or dolphin,
        no playful mammal of the deep.

Despite appearance, this one skulks in caverns
sunk below my sight,
        familiar with the paths of underworld
        yet surfacing from time to time
        with small and greedy eyes.

I'm almost sure it maps with care, maybe for days on end,
my spinning bark,
heaving the waters hard against the prow
to thrust it clear of shorelines:

        northwards or south to where the ice
        swims in eternal midnight beneath a narrow moon.

Fallen Lorikeet

This one image of you
will abide the rest:

the morning you came to my door
carrying a fallen lorikeet,
its partner dead in the East Garden,
        its beak smashed,
        the small brain damaged beyond repair.

We sit together on the door-step
pondering what to do—
you are already late for work
but dismiss it with a shrug—

the bird in its distress and plumage
(a creature flown from paradise
into hard, unseeing glass)
is cupped in your dark hands,
raised high,
        the purple head, the long green tail,
        the bleeding though still dangerous beak,
stilled by your voice
and long, unwavering fingers:
        a pool of serenity and light.

Cradled and comforted,
living or dead,
you hold the wounded bird
with all the bearing
of a sparrow in its father's hands.

Boat Scene

Sometimes in the sleepless drift
of dawn you see
yourself afloat
in latitude on any one of seven
seas, the waves defying
strokes and mounting upwards,
the coracle
rocked on either side, soaked
to the skin in brine, the irate winds
    hurling your tiny, wooden
    world downwards
    to a soggy bed.

You don't give in, of course, fighting
to turn a rain-drenched gaze
elsewhere, upwards perhaps beyond the rising
waters and the lowering
clouds, the dark line of their meeting,
past unimaginable stars —

    to wonder if a lunar eye
    beholds the pounding waves;
    and what the chance
    of some sprite emissary striding
    towards you on the open sea.

Cosmos

You sit at the table in the dining-room,
crossing your legs and clasping a mug of tea,
ready to impart your latest erudition:

a book about celestial space, you say,
fields of the universe uncomputed,
curling on distant borders,
forming a dome light-years above.

(Ironically, a colder and less friendly
sky than what the ancients knew —
windows and doors flung open day by day
for congress with the deity
dwelling above in splendid company)

The traveller, you speculate, even at the speed of light
might journey year by year
and reach at best the thinning out of galaxies,
the mind drained dry
by disconnected sights.

When at last the monologue is over,
you rise to take departure,
leaving us ruminating at all the signs
paraded in your cool, prosaic way;

standing in the doorway in a pool of lunar light,
we glimpse for a moment far above
the patient, glimmering stars;

turning to face an interior constellation,
a museum of fractured wonders
every bit as vast.

Shallows

I seem to be splashing round in shallows,
in tangy waves of spring
        that push themselves against the sands,
        their coolness reaching to my waist.

I'll hardly tell you where I am or why.

Perhaps I should be somewhere else entirely,
but here, for now, there's comfort in the billows:

hoping one day a boat will knock against me,
willed by a voice along the shore:

        make me a captive in a Galilean dragnet
        wedged in a catch of fish,
        tailored to each fine fin and scale.

Night Travels

At night you travel quickly,
the pavements bare,
the roads sleek
        from midnight showers
        or ponderous street-sweepers.

Remembering half-heard tales —
of strangers and headlights
that have no destiny but yours.

South of the city,
the lamps are too dim to reach
the buildings or the shadows.
You're alone without defence,
        as if a child has grasped your imprint
        in a picture,
        cutting it out and setting it aside.

Strangest of all the impression
that, just around the corner,
a company has passed,

and all that's left is only an indentation,
        a distant tinkling of bells
        receding further and further
        down the dewy street —

dancing in shadowed air
you wouldn't even dare to breathe.

Baptisms

The river is brown.
It threatens to burst its banks
from last night's rains.
    Small birds skim the surface of the water,
    dipping their wings
    and ruffling the current's harried pace.

I used to swim this river in my childhood,
safe in the willow's antique shade
its fingers trailing on the ripples —
fixed at the shallowest point
    where you could wade on sweltering days
    beneath a burning firmament.

Once long ago a stranger declined to bathe
rejecting the River Jordan,
asking instead for lucid streams
with fish and stones and gardens,
in wistfulness for home;
    his ailing form at last with his consent
    rising unsullied in the moonlight.

And once when clouds were looming,
another I heard of sank beneath these waves,
heedless of wind and rain,
a bird in wheeling flight above.
He struck out down-stream for the current,
meeting the river's haste,
his dark head bobbing among the rocks.

Then perched for an instant on the world's edge,
holding against the fall with arms extended,
he vanished in the furious foam.

They saw him later rising from the waters
his face turned upwards to the sky.

Today I stand on the muddy verge,
scanning the secrets these stories hold:
for the river,
for me,
for everyone.

Planet

The night like the days is sultry,
a fine wind stirs.
The smell of grasses burning in the north
invades the air.
The dome of evening stages a half moon
holding sublimely centre space,
companioned by the planet Jupiter.
        They will pass each other slowly
        in silent circles of the night.

For most other beings in the city,
in this converging night,
sleep will be evasive;
and we will wake, and wake again,
in clammy perspiration.

For now I sit and contemplate
within the dimming firmament
the arduous day just past:
the knowledge of a task that falters.

        Wishing I might live as quiet
        as the darkening sky,
        beyond the acrid stench,
        holding serenely to my tended course:

passing by moons and planets
in cool but courteous dance.

3

Mythic Poems

Ariadne 1

I stand on the shores facing the waves,
shivering in the salt spray.
It is five weeks since I came.
Each day the white foam is my only visitor,
tumbling towards me in its haste,
just as he once fell into my arms.

Then at once the waves recede,
to merge with the distant places he has gone,
carrying his bark to a higher destiny.

> (I was the labyrinthine key,
> the thread that saved him from a monstrous fate,
> He wound the thread around the spindle,
> weaving my veins into the fabric of his need.)

If I look up at the dome above,
perhaps I might trace the nascent eye
of some discerning god,
the contours of a face, divinely sad,
> ready to observe, to count the tears,
> to scribe the unseen pain.

For now, I stand forlorn upon the shore.
Only the bright waves beckon and depart,
promise and betray,
yearning, shrinking, living, dying.
I embrace as home this place where,
day after day,
I play out the drama of desire and loss:
> a broken shard,
> a foundering ship,
> a wounded seagull reeling through the gale.

Ariadne 2

Today I hold your image in my hands:
flecked on the small, dark vase you left behind
when first you came to visit me.

You recline on clay,
black lines etched in a circle of light.
You are the guest of honour at this banquet hour,
your body naked beneath the wispy cloth,
grave and solemn in reflection
while everything whirls around you
    In the distance your ship resides at anchor,
    tendrils coiled around the bows, the mast, the upright prow.
    Dolphins revel in the sea.

Day after day, your likeness teaches me the same:
that loss and departure are not all one.

I know you will return.
That's why I trace the inner meaning of your form.
I understand the silence,
finding the weight of bliss cannot be held for long
in mortal hands.

And now at last I can be free:
    drink wine from an earthen kantharos,
    twine ivy leaves around my head,
    run barefoot on the glistening sands,

training myself through flight
for incandescent glory.

Persephone

I. She sits on a rock
        pensive in the deepening sunlight.
        She is a goddess, Demeter's child,
        given for this moment to rise above the world.
        She hums a tune;
        breathes in the tangled flowers in her lap.

In the valleys, the bright corn ripens.
A small cloud gathers on the rim.

II. Deep in the earth's bowels,
she comes at last to the Underworld.
The goddess she loves is gone.

There is no knowledge to compare with this,
down at the heart's core:
        'I am the living dead entombed in deathly arms,
        'I am the source of winter'.

Was this the darkness she longed for
on those temperate nights of long ago:
        the lover's arms,
        the strong soft flesh,
        the ecstasy of presence?

'O for the bright world once again,
'O for the goddess who plants the seeds!'

The world above her lies in mourning.

III. It's a long road across the waste land.
I leave behind the winter,
taking the pathway to Spring,
to those who await my appearing;

all through the summer months
rejoicing in the harvest of your labours;

never forgetting the echoing hall,
 the dark and wintry god,
 the seeded fruit that beckons me.

I gain subsistence on this loop of life and death:
at once both lost and found,
dispersed and gathered in.

Antigone

You always were my favourite:
    your pathway clear,
    courage beyond your culture.

Defying the king,
turning your back on your betrothed;

revering the gods
and mysteries of the Underworld,
you dared to bury your brother
— despite the penalty.

How tall you stood back then
against the expectations of your gender.

How strong you still appear,
    a woman among women
    for your and every other time.

Elektra

Trapped like a rabbit,
she turns this way and that,
        not knowing how to break free
        or if freedom is even possible.

Unlike her parents,
fighters both and warriors
— against the world and against each other —
she is timorous and gentle.

If she loves anyone
it is the brother
who cares for and considers her;

but is tormented.
She understands the rage.

Yet how to escape
the violence and the hatred?
        How not to end up confined
        forever
        within their feuding ranks?

She longs for someone, anyone
to unfetter her
so she can nurse the heartache
        in the deep burrows
        of her solitude.

Kassandra

I. I am a prophet
sprung from kingly blood,
fated
never to be believed.

Was I a fool to spurn the advances
of the god
whose fury and whose curse
have overshadowed me?

With one hand he gave a gift
and with the other took it.

When I cried out in protest
no-one heeded.
I spoke aloud but was as silent as the grave.

II. This time again I have no speech:
the captive of a king
and his success in bloodshed.

Behind me lies the city of my birth:
my family, status, dignity — all gone.

Before me spreads the township
on an outcrop,
its stones and gate and curving walls,
its priests and architects,
the pride of its refinement.

And now we stand before the palace,

the queen awaiting with the one I know
to be her lover.

They spread a carpet
for his triumph,
red as the blood I know they'll shed
the moment he walks across the threshold.

I cry out the silent warning of a slave:

    not only his but mine.

www.ingramcontent.com/pod-product-compliance
Lightning Source LLC
Chambersburg PA
CBHW011954090526
44591CB00020B/2763

* 9 7 8 1 9 2 2 5 8 9 4 4 6 *